I0839335

Sending you joyful hugs this Easter.

May all of your dreams

and wishes come true.

smile eggs
Happy
Easter
sun
love
HAPPY
EGG
life
bunny
joy
good
chicken
spring

Mommy,

Wishing you an Easter that is bright,

happy, and full of contentment.

Hoppy Easter!

Sand-hill Cranes, Robins, and Red winged
blackbirds will sing,
Meeting together for the arrival of spring!

Hope your Easter is bright with color,

sweet with treats, and warm with sunshine!

Easter

Mommy,

May the hope of spring
bring days that are filled with joy,
laughter, and good times!

Wishing you an Easter that is as sweet
and special as you are!

Easter is more than just eggs and candy.
It is also about peace, love, and family.

Mommy,
I'm thinking of you and wishing you a
warm and wonderful bunny day!

Delivering hugs, kisses, and Easter
wishes just for you!

Thinking of you this season of renewal
& wishing you happiness at Easter &
throughout the year.

Here's hoping your spring is filled with the beauty of nature.

Copyright 2018 by florabella publishing.

All rights reserved. No part of this book may be

reproduced in any form or by any electronic means

including information storage and

retrieval systems, without permission in writing from

the authors. The only exception is by a reviewer,

whom may quote short excerpts in a review.

from Florabella Publishing, LLC

www.ingramcontent.com/pod-product-compliance
Lightning Source LLC
Chambersburg PA
CBHW061925270726
48659CB00002BA/933